Slices of Life
with Peanut Butter

Poems © 2019 Amy Houchen
Illustrations © 2019 Allie Sullberg

Text © 2019 by Amy Houchen
Illustrations © 2019 by Allie Sullberg

All rights reserved. No part of this publication may be reproduced or distributed in any form or by any means, or stored in a database or retrieval system, without the prior written permission of the author.

ISBN: 978-0-578-52199-2

Evening Off the Morning

At breakfast time I play the game
of making stuff come out the same.
With syrup on French toast and such,
I almost always pour too much.
So when I've polished this one off I'll
have to have another waffle.

It's not too challenging with jam
'cause I can almost always cram
a little more on bread or toast,
whichever kind I like the most.

But cereal is more demanding:
I add milk, it starts expanding!
Who knows when I begin the bowl
if they'll be even? That's my goal.

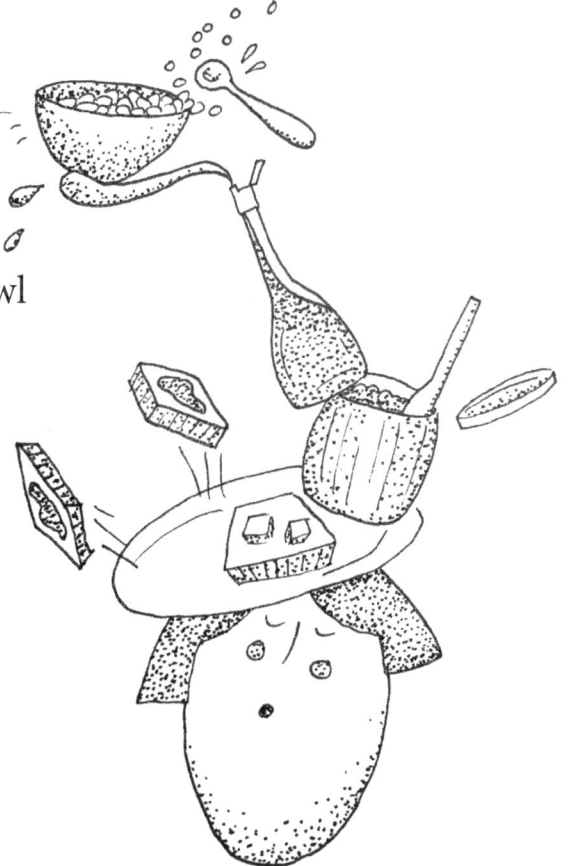

The Third Syrup

Perhaps you have searched through the cupboards and fridge
for your favorite syrup and can't find a smidge
of chocolate or maple, but that's not defeat.
Now try the third syrup that's both brown and sweet.
Just reach for molasses. Oh, you heard me right.
You may not have known that it makes every bite
of French toast or waffles or pancakes taste great
right after you've buttered them, stacked on your plate.
It also is yummy when mixed in with milk,
transforming your glassful to liquid brown silk.

The Vegetable Plot

My zucchinis like it when the weather's hot
as they sunbathe in a vegetable plot.

Tomatoes and potatoes right next door
are ripening for my soup du jour.

Green peas are hiding in pods near the ground,
crossing their tendrils they won't be found.

Once peppers turn orange, yellow and red,
it's time that they got out of bed.

The second row over has sprung a few leeks
that can't be fixed for weeks and weeks.

My cabbage has heads but they can't hear;
they ask the corn to lend an ear.

Eggplants hatch purple, green and white
without a single hen in sight.

As garlic keeps evil spirits away,
the celery stalks toward the relish tray.

But if you want okra, beets and chard,
you'll have to grow them in your own yard.

The Artist

I have so many art utensils—
look at all my colored pencils,
crayons, markers by the dozen,
and more paper than my cousin.

Why can't I make my pictures look
as good as any in a book?
My parents are no help; they say
they'd rather see mine any day.

Persistence

When I feel that little jiggle
telling me a tooth is loose,
I try my hardest to ignore it
but just trying is no use.

When both my tongue and fingers
find that they can make it budge
they start to jostle, shake and poke
and then they twist and nudge.

But after they've succeeded—
even when the fairy's paid—
my fingers will forget the gap;
my tongue will still invade.

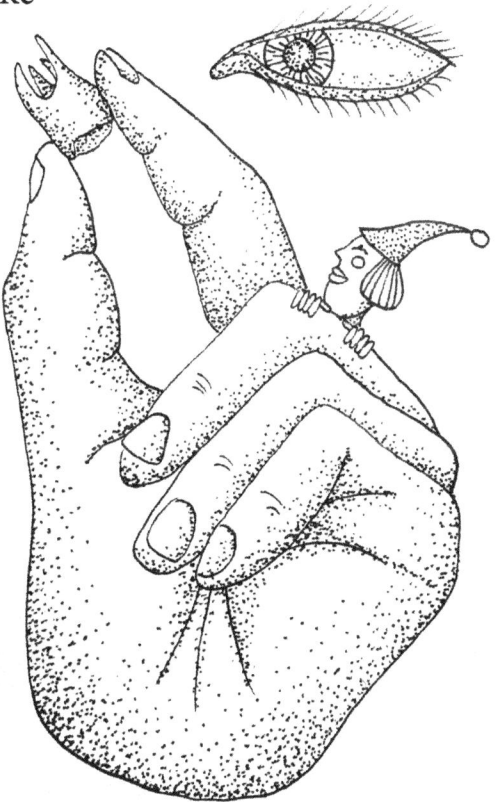

New House Blues

I don't know why my parents think
that our new house is fine.
It may be their perfect home
but it sure isn't mine.

I wish they could have found a house
that has a dusty attic
full of trunks and books in code
'cause then I'd be ecstatic.

My closet walls are clean and smooth.
I've looked but I can't see
a panel I could press to find
a secret room for me.

This house is on one level.
It has no laundry chute
or cellar floor to excavate
for pirates' buried loot.

I now live inside a house
that's no good for exploring.
I should ask a ghost to come
and make this place less boring.

Blackberries

My mom makes better blackberry pie
than any you could ever buy.
She also makes great blackberry jam
which is the best, of that I am
as sure as I am of these scratches.
How d'you think she makes those batches?
I'm the one who has to pick
the berries from the vines that stick
and even if I haven't bled
my hands are always stained bright red.
So I have helped to pay the price
for all that stuff that tastes so nice.

Transposing Ts

You may be one of those, like me,
who adds an extra letter T,
allowing it to intervene
when saying numbers like four[t-]teen.

Those extra T's are lying low
in words where we don't say them. Though
seen in castle and in glisten,
you can't hear them when you listen.

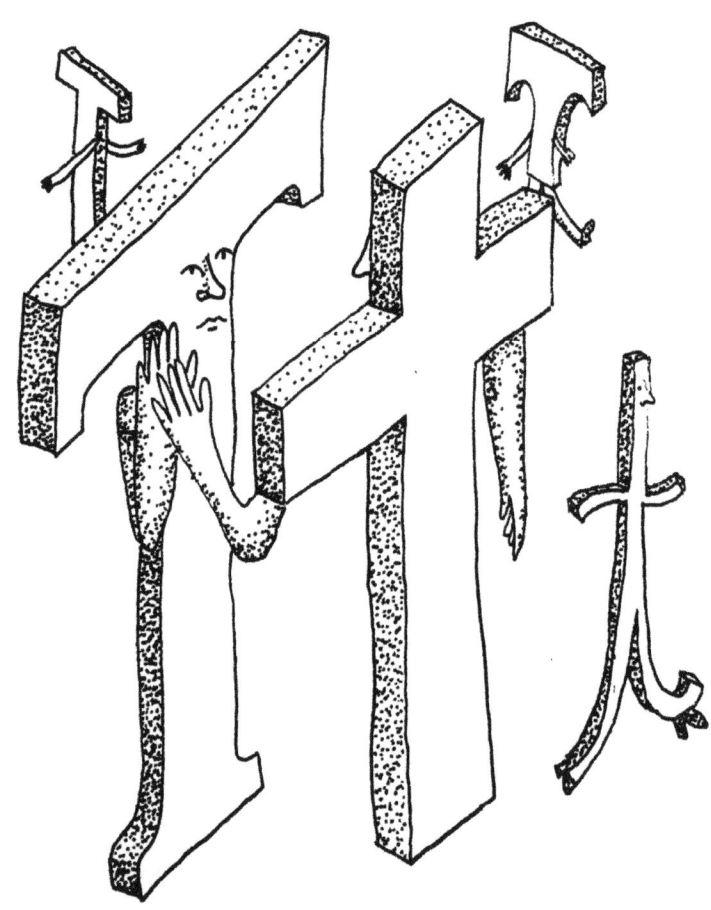

Destroying the Evidence

Now that I am getting tall
the most inviting square of wall
that's just above the kitchen door
may not entice me as before.

Someday I won't have the fun
of leaping when I'm on the run
and slapping it with all my might
which I do every time despite
the fact I must then scrub it clean
of proof that I'm a jump machine.

Decisions

Tomato soup along with cheese—
now that's a lunch that's sure to please.
But every time I must decide
just how to get the cheese inside.
If I put cubes in with the soup
they melt and flavor every scoop,
yet sometimes I want cheese on bread.
So, toasted? Maybe grilled instead.

The Umble Family

Next door to me lives a family named Umble.
They're proud of being incessantly humble.
That's just as well, for each, it turns out,
has some little quirk to be humble about.

Joseph, the youngest, seems always to fumble
whatever you throw him and then takes a tumble
but as luck would have it, never so badly
that one of his somersaults ever ends sadly.

Ernest, the middle kid, likely will stumble
on things that aren't there, and his stomach will rumble
even at times when it's good to be quiet.
I think he needs to go on a sound diet.

And Blossom, the eldest, may speak in a mumble
or else so quickly her words are a jumble.
It's not that she doesn't have plenty to say;
it's just that her words tend to get in the way.

But now that I think of it, I sometimes bumble.
Maybe I'm being unfair when I grumble
so much about them; it might just turn out
that I have some quirks they all grumble about.

Boxes

I like mint boxes made of tin,
just right to keep my stickers in.
A bigger chocolate box I'll smell
until it's so old I can't tell
what it once held, and then I'll stow
some things I don't want kids to know
about because they'd wreck my stuff
by handling it a bit too rough.
Sometimes I use a pencil box.
I wish that it had come with locks.

The rubber stamp that looks like feet,
the flash drive I found on the street,
this gray and purple keychain gnome:
my little treasures need a home.
These things I need to organize
so no one has the bad surprise
of stepping on my dark brass ring
or any other tiny thing
that I keep hidden safe away
until I bring it out to play.

When I get boxes with clear tops
I round up teeny things for props.
I'll pave the roads with dominoes,
then paint inside so that it shows
just where my pint-sized highways run.
There's more to do before I'm done;
I'll color golf tees brown and green
to be the trees inside my scene.
I never have a box too many—
do you want to give me any?

The Best Driveway

I'm boasting. Ours is really good:
by far the best in the neighborhood,
with no rough paving, bumpy seams
or slopes to spoil my driveway dreams.

It's a hopscotch course, it's a roller rink,
and also just the spot, I think,
for bashing tennis balls at the door
until my arms are tired and sore.

It has a basketball hoop, of course;
my friends and I keep playing HORSE
until we can't quite see the rim
because the sky has grown so dim.

Although it's not the biggest space,
it truly is my favorite place:
the perfect site for outdoor schemes
despite how flat and gray it seems.

The Last Straw

My favorite sweatshirt is a hoodie.
Although it's old it's still a goodie.
This big brown stain appeared way back
the day I had an ice cream snack.

That's when a piece of chocolate shell
broke off the bottom, and it fell
right here and melted. I forgot
to wash it soon and so this spot

lives on now right beside the rip
that happened as I tried to slip
beneath a fence and caught a nail
that stuck out from the lowest rail.

Now it's shredding into tatters
but that's not what really matters
since the zipper still can close.
Once broken, out my hoodie goes.

Eating Outside the Box

Just this one time, can we please
make a different mac and cheese?
At Taylor's house they never use
the kind in boxes. No, they choose
to dump cooked noodles in a pan
and grate as much cheese as they can;
then mix it in, and next they pour
the right amount of milk—not more
than halfway up the cheesy stuff.
Melt butter. Crumble in enough
saltines to sprinkle on the top.
Bake until it's time to stop:
when the cracker crumbs are browned
and milk no longer slops around.
The very tastiest part of it's
the top and bottom crusty bits.

Muffin-tin Meals

On days I'm feeling sick and yucky
normal food has no appeal.
But when it's time to eat, I'm lucky—
Mom gives me a muffin-tin meal.

Six little cups of different foods—
banana, yogurt, crackers, cheese,
some grapes and carrots—fit my mood.
A bit of each is plenty, please.

Oh, you may say I'm like a baby
but you shouldn't be so quick
to slam it. Try it; I think maybe
you would like it when you're sick.

That's right: don't underestimate
just how much better you will feel
when rather than a dinner plate
you're treated to a muffin-tin meal!

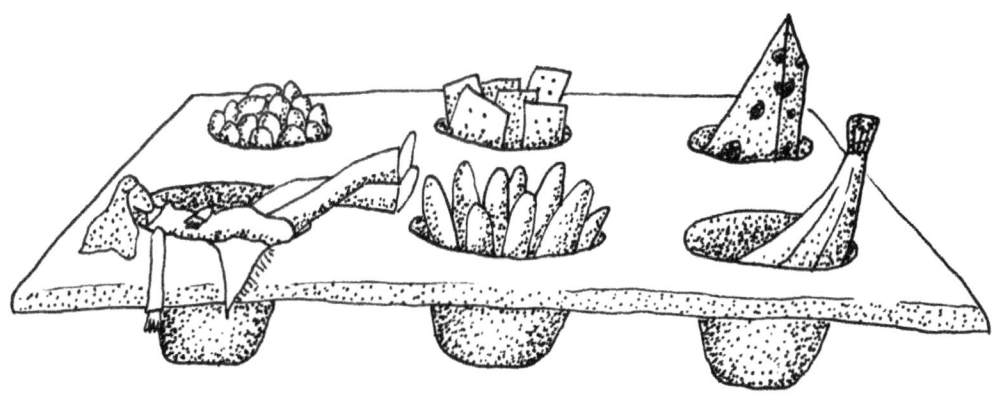

Wildlife

There used to be an old raccoon
that came up on our deck.
It had three legs and just one ear—
it seemed to be a wreck.

But it was tough and wouldn't leave
no matter how we yelled.
So just how did my family get
that old raccoon expelled?

I must confess it wasn't us
who made it disappear;
I'd guess it was the coyotes
who showed up late last year.

They might not come up on the deck
but I have heard them yowl.
They yip until I'm wide awake—
and then I want to howl!

Magnificent Magnolia

Her magnificent magnolia
is my mom's favorite tree.
She says when it blooms pink and white
it's lovely as can be.

That magnificent magnolia
is great, without a doubt.
I'd say that even if no flowers
ever did pop out.

What makes that tree magnificent
is how the branches grow—
they're not very far apart
and they start really low.

So if you are just starting out
to learn how to climb trees,
a magnificent magnolia
will make your task a breeze.

Peanut Butter

I'm quite attached to peanut butter.
Any kid can tell you what're
downsides of my favorite spread;
it's worst when smeared alone on bread.
The glue effect can make me mutter—
limit me to just a sputter.
But I don't tire of its taste
or of the fact it must be chased
with milk to make my throat a hollow
so I once again can swallow.

Respect for Dirt

My parents say, "We beg your pardon;
what's called earth out in the garden
turns to dirt on hands and neck.
Indoors, we give it no respect.
So scrub it off, and don't complain;
just send it all right down the drain."
They could return that dirt to earth,
outside where it would have some worth.
They don't realize they could hose
me off between the garden rows.

Composing Compost

When filling up the compost bin,
what sort of stuff should you throw in?

Broccoli trimmings limp and green,
one last dreary lima bean;
moldy pasta, tired toast,
salad that gave up the ghost,
flowers that have passed their primes,
rinds of lemons and of limes.

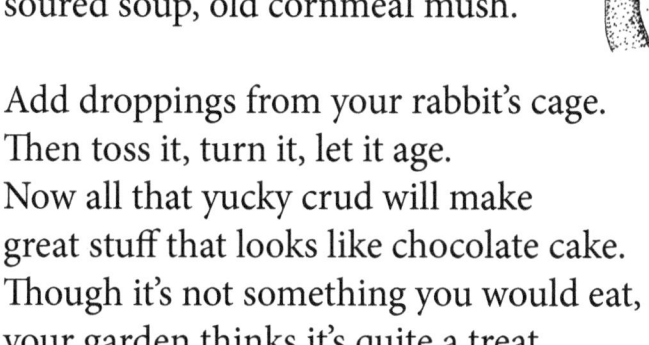

Don't forget the dryer lint,
spuds with an unsavory tint,
clippings from the shrubs and lawn,
apples that are too far gone,
hair from cleaning out your brush,
soured soup, old cornmeal mush.

Add droppings from your rabbit's cage.
Then toss it, turn it, let it age.
Now all that yucky crud will make
great stuff that looks like chocolate cake.
Though it's not something you would eat,
your garden thinks it's quite a treat.

Serpentine Sonnet

Eighteen damascene
    aubergine snakes
        reverently resting
           around the rakes,
              or slithering, dithering
           on withering sod,
      noiselessly, nakedly
          with nary a nod;
              curious, spurious,
                  penurious adders
                      lackadaisically lounging
                  under the ladders
              until coiling, roiling,
          toiling on land:
          a bald, bodacious
              and bilious band;
                  serpents with haughty
                      thoughts of knots,
                        flexibly flirting
                  near the flowerpots;
              worrying, scurrying,
            hurrying along edges,
          in sliding scales
        along the hedges;
      somehow seeming
similar to snails—
    are they
      almost
        all necks,
          or almost
        all tails?

My Next Birthday Party

Not the usual birthday party.
Nothing rented, nothing arty.
We've been swimming,
we've gone skating,
we've done lots of celebrating.
There won't be time to fly to Mars
or past a couple nearby stars.
Of course we need ice cream and cake,
so we'll just spend the time to make
those. And since I'm the birthday child
you know the flavors will be wild!

The Longcut

"It's just a couple blocks," my friend told me.
"A shortcut. It will take less time. You'll see."

But after making four wrong turns I found
a shortcut can be very long around.

Training Ground

You may think I'm crazy
because I volunteer
to vacuum all the carpet
but wait until you hear:

it's practice for the future
when I'm old enough to mow
our lawn just like an outfield,
as if I were a pro.

One week I'll carve our lawn in stripes,
another in curved lines,
and when I feel creative,
I'll sculpt my own designs.

They'll look great, I guarantee,
until the weather calls "Strike three!"

Guardian

Above my books, on my top shelf,
there lives my little wooden elf
(not a dwarf or garden gnome).
I hope it likes its lofty home
where it can fend off every beast
who thinks I'd make a tasty feast.
So monsters, orcs and trolls beware:
my elf can stop you with its stare.

My room is dark and scary, so
on nights I want a friendly glow
I just turn on my bedside light
named Mr. Moon, who's not too bright.
His top curve holds a smiling star
named Kansas. I am glad they are
nearby so I can check to see
my elf still standing guard for me.

Weeding

Grass in flowerbeds,
ivy out of bounds;
trees that squirrels planted,
morning-glory mounds.
I'm supposed to yank out
all these weeds
before my parents
begin sowing seeds.

And always dandelions
growing in the lawn.
I bet they'll never be
totally gone.
Come and see me
when I'm ninety-two.
I'll still be weeding,
my whole life through.

Top Shelf Trouble

I didn't do it—
don't blame me.
It's so far back
I couldn't see

the jar that now
has grayish stuff.
I think it's lived there
long enough.

The fridge is not
a happy place
when food has whiskers
on its face.

This Time of Night

About this time
every night
I try to stay
out of sight.

I got all
my homework done
but didn't finish
all the fun
things I hoped
I'd do before
my parents say:
"Now it's your

bedtime."

Hiding Places

I've outgrown my hiding places.
I don't fit inside those spaces
like below the kitchen sink.
Sometimes I wish that I could shrink.
It's all my fault Mom put a damper
on my hiding in the hamper;
I broke it once.

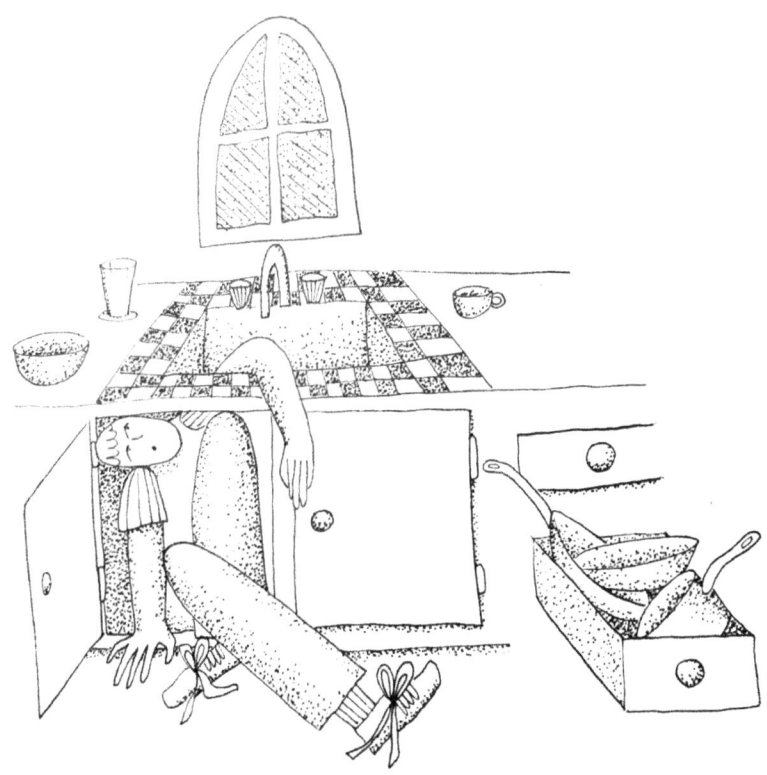

I'm very thorough—
I've found every place to burrow.
Since I know each space to stash
stuff in my house, where is the cache
of gifts? We're almost to December.
I just hope my folks remember.

Bed Threads

I'm choosy when I hit the hay
'cause I don't want a plain duvet.
Too often when it's on I'm hot
and then too chilly when it's not.
So give me sheets and blankets, please.
That way I'll neither cook nor freeze.
When it's so warm in late July
just one smooth sheet may satisfy,
but on a cool May night I might
decide a cotton blanket, light
and soft, is what I need to pull
up so I'm snug. In winter, wool
with flannel sheets is cozy. Still,
if my skin's burning when I'm ill
it might as well be summer then
as I'll want just smooth sheets again.

Mystery

I don't know why
so many kids
think top bunks are appealing.

It's no big deal
just to have
your nose next to the ceiling.

Scary Nights

The nights when I'm too scared to try
to sleep I want a lullaby,
'cause one I haven't heard since maybe
back when I was just a baby
helps a lot when I'm upset;
I feel safer and forget.

Don't tell my friends.
They'd roll their eyes,
say they're not scared
and other lies.

ISBN 978-0-578-52199-2

90000>

www.ingramcontent.com/pod-product-compliance
Lightning Source LLC
Chambersburg PA
CBHW061801290426
44109CB00030B/2914